KU-166-440

ESSENTIAL
Potatoes

Contents

Introduction

The potato originated in South America and is thought to date back as far as 3000 BC. First known as the *papa* and eaten by the Incas, it was unknown to the rest of the world until the sixteenth century when the Spanish Conquistador Francisco Pizarro captured Peru.

The potato was not readily accepted in Europe, however, because it was known to be a member of the nightshade family and therefore thought to be poisonous. It first arrived via Spain and its name gradually changed from *papa* to *battata*. Once it was acknowledged for both its nutritional and healing properties – the Italians believed it could heal a wound if the cooked flesh was rubbed in to the infected area – it spread to Belgium, Germany, Switzerland and France.

It was not until Sir Frances Drake stopped in the New World and shared his cargo of potatoes with the starving colonists that the potato was introduced to the British Isles. Later repatriated by Sir Walter Raleigh, the colonists brought the potato to Britain. Raleigh was instrumental in destroying the poisonous potato superstition by taking the potato to Ireland and successfully growing it on his own land. The Irish soon adopted the potato as their own and it became a mainstay of their diet.

There are about 3000 known varieties of potato but only about 100 of them are regularly grown. Each type of potato is suitable for different cooking methods, whether it be steaming, baking, mashing or frying.

What makes it particularly versatile is the fact that it absorbs other flavours readily and it has a consistency that lends itself to many uses.

On average we each eat 109 kg/242 lb of potatoes per annum. The average 225 g/8 oz potato contains 180 calories, protein, starch for energy and fibre, as well as being a good source of vitamin C. Most vitamins are found just beneath the skin of potatoes, which is why it is often suggested that they are cooked in their skins and then peeled.

When choosing and using potatoes check that they are firm, regular-shaped, either red or yellow in colour and have a smooth, tight skin. Avoid potatoes which are turning green or sprouting, as the flavour will be bitter and they will have higher levels of the natural toxicants called glycaolkaloids. Store potatoes in a cool, dark, dry place, as too much light will turn them green.

The selection of recipes in this book range from hearty soups and salads to main meals and beautiful bakes, all made from that humble, and most delicious of staple foods, the potato. There is something for everyone – whether you are on a diet, a vegetarian or just a potato lover.

Sweet Potato & Onion Soup

Serves 4

INGREDIENTS

2 tbsp vegetable oil
900 g/2 lb sweet potatoes, diced
1 carrot, diced
2 onions, sliced
2 garlic cloves, crushed
600 ml/1 pint/2¹/₂ cups vegetable
stock

300 ml/¹/₂ pint/1¹/₄ cups
unsweetened orange juice
225 ml/8 fl oz/1 cup natural
yogurt
2 tbsp chopped fresh coriander
(cilantro)
salt and pepper

TO GARNISH:
coriander (cilantro) sprigs
orange rind

1 Heat the vegetable oil in a large saucepan and add the diced sweet potatoes and carrot, sliced onions and garlic. Sauté gently for 5 minutes, stirring constantly.

2 Pour in the vegetable stock and orange juice and bring them to the boil.

3 Reduce the heat to a simmer, cover the saucepan and cook the vegetables for 20 minutes or until the sweet potato and carrot cubes are tender.

4 Transfer the mixture to a food processor or blender in batches and process for 1 minute until puréed. Return the purée to the rinsed-out saucepan.

5 Stir in the natural yogurt and chopped coriander (cilantro) and season to taste. Serve the soup garnished with coriander (cilantro) sprigs and orange rind.

COOK'S TIP

This soup can be chilled before serving, if preferred. If chilling it, stir the yogurt into the dish just before serving. Serve in chilled bowls.

Indian Potato & Pea Soup

Serves 4

INGREDIENTS

2 tbsp vegetable oil
225 g/8 oz floury (mealy)
    potatoes, diced
1 large onion, chopped
2 garlic cloves, crushed
1 tsp garam masala

1 tsp ground coriander
1 tsp ground cumin
900 ml/1$\frac{1}{2}$ pints/3$\frac{3}{4}$cups
    vegetable stock
1 red chilli, chopped
100 g/3$\frac{1}{2}$ oz frozen peas

4 tbsp natural yogurt
salt and pepper
chopped fresh coriander
    (cilantro), to garnish

1 Heat the vegetable oil in a large saucepan and add the diced potatoes, onion and garlic. Sauté gently for about 5 minutes, stirring constantly.

2 Add the ground spices and cook for 1 minute, stirring all the time.

3 Stir in the vegetable stock and chopped red chilli and bring the mixture to the boil. Reduce the heat, cover the pan and simmer for 20 minutes until the potatoes begin to break down.

4 Add the peas and cook for a further 5 minutes. Stir in the yogurt and season to taste.

5 Pour into warmed soup bowls, garnish with chopped fresh coriander (cilantro) and serve hot with warm bread.

COOK'S TIP

Potatoes blend perfectly with spices, this soup being no exception. For an authentic Indian dish, serve this soup with warm naan bread.

VARIATION

For slightly less heat, deseed the chilli before adding it to the soup. Always wash your hands after handling chillies as they contain volatile oils that can irritate the skin and make your eyes burn if you touch your face.

Potato, Rocket (Arugula) & Apple Salad

Serves 4

INGREDIENTS

2 large potatoes, unpeeled and sliced
2 green dessert apples, diced
1 tsp lemon juice
25 g/1 oz walnut pieces
125 g/4½ oz goat's cheese, cubed

150 g/5½ oz rocket (arugula) leaves
salt and pepper

DRESSING:
2 tbsp olive oil
1 tbsp red wine vinegar

1 tsp clear honey
1 tsp fennel seeds

1 Cook the potatoes in a pan of boiling water for 15 minutes until tender. Drain and leave to cool. Transfer the cooled potatoes to a serving bowl.

2 Toss the diced apples in the lemon juice, drain and stir into the cold potatoes.

3 Add the walnut pieces, cheese cubes and rocket (arugula) leaves, then toss the salad to mix.

4 In a small bowl, whisk the dressing ingredients together and pour the dressing over the salad. Serve immediately.

VARIATION

Use smoked or blue cheese instead of goat's cheese, if you prefer. In addition, if rocket (arugula) is unavailable use baby spinach instead.

COOK'S TIP

Serve this salad immediately to prevent the apple from discolouring. Alternatively, prepare all of the other ingredients in advance and add the apple at the last minute.

Grilled (Broiled) New Potato Salad

Serves 4

INGREDIENTS

650 g/1½ lb new potatoes,
    scrubbed
3 tbsp olive oil
2 tbsp chopped fresh thyme
1 tsp paprika
4 rashers smoked bacon

salt and pepper
parsley sprig, to garnish

DRESSING:
4 tbsp mayonnaise
1 tbsp garlic wine vinegar

2 garlic cloves, crushed
1 tbsp chopped fresh parsley

1 Cook the new potatoes in a saucepan of boiling water for 10 minutes. Drain thoroughly.

2 Mix the olive oil, chopped thyme and paprika together and pour the mixture over the warm potatoes.

3 Place the bacon rashers under a preheated medium grill (broiler) and cook for 5 minutes, turning once until crisp. When cooked, roughly chop the bacon and keep warm.

4 Transfer the potatoes to the grill (broiler) pan and cook for 10 minutes, turning once.

5 Mix the dressing ingredients in a small serving bowl. Transfer the potatoes and bacon to a large serving bowl. Season with salt and pepper and mix together.

6 Spoon over the dressing, garnish with a parsley sprig and serve immediately for a warm salad. Alternatively, leave to cool and serve chilled.

VARIATION

Add spicy sausage to the salad in place of bacon – you do not need to cook it under the grill (broiler) before adding to the salad.

Potato & Italian Sausage Salad

Serves 4

INGREDIENTS

450 g/1 lb waxy potatoes
1 raddichio or lollo rosso lettuce
1 green (bell) pepper, sliced
175 g/6 oz Italian sausage, sliced
1 red onion, halved and sliced

125 g/4¹/₂ oz sun-dried
   tomatoes, sliced
2 tbsp shredded fresh basil

DRESSING:
1 tbsp balsamic vinegar
1 tsp tomato purée (paste)
2 tbsp olive oil
salt and pepper

1 Cook the potatoes in a saucepan of boiling water for 20 minutes or until cooked through. Drain and leave to cool.

2 Line a large serving platter with the radicchio or lollo rosso lettuce leaves.

3 Slice the cooled potatoes and arrange them in layers on the lettuce-lined serving platter together with the sliced green (bell) pepper, sliced Italian sausage, red onion, sun-dried tomatoes and shredded fresh basil.

4 In a small bowl, whisk the balsamic vinegar, tomato purée (paste) and olive oil together and season to taste with salt and pepper. Pour the dressing over the potato salad and serve immediately.

COOK'S TIP

You can use either packets of sun-dried tomatoes or jars of sun-dried tomatoes in oil. If using tomatoes packed in oil, simply rinse the oil from the tomatoes and pat them dry on paper towels before using.

VARIATION

Any sliced Italian sausage or salami can be used in this salad. Italy is home of the salami and there are numerous varieties to choose from – those from the south tend to be more highly spiced than those from the north of the country.

Smoked Fish & Potato Pâté

Serves 4

INGREDIENTS

650 g/1½ lb floury (mealy)
    potatoes, diced
300 g/10½ oz smoked mackerel,
    skinned and flaked
75 g/2¾ oz cooked gooseberries

2 tsp lemon juice
2 tbsp crème fraîche
1 tbsp capers
1 gherkin, chopped
1 tbsp chopped dill pickle

1 tbsp chopped fresh dill
salt and pepper
lemon wedges, to garnish

1 Cook the diced potatoes in a saucepan of boiling water for 10 minutes until tender, then drain well.

2 Place the cooked potatoes in a food processor or blender.

3 Add the skinned and flaked smoked mackerel and process for 30 seconds until fairly smooth. Alternatively, mash with a fork.

4 Add the cooked gooseberries with the lemon juice and crème fraîche. Blend for a further 10 seconds or mash well.

5 Stir in the capers, gherkin, dill pickle and chopped fresh dill. Season well with salt and pepper.

6 Turn the fish pâté into a serving dish, garnish with lemon wedges and serve with slices of toast or warm crusty bread in chunks or slices.

COOK'S TIP

Use stewed, canned or bottled cooked gooseberries for convenience and to save time, or when fresh gooseberries are out of season.

VARIATION

Use other tart fruits, such as stewed apples, instead of the gooseberries if they are unavailable.

Potato Kibbeh

Serves 4

INGREDIENTS

175 g/6 oz bulgar wheat	pinch of grated nutmeg	1 tbsp pine kernels (nuts)
350 g/12 oz floury (mealy)	salt and pepper	25 g/1 oz dried apricots, chopped
potatoes, diced	oil for deep-frying	pinch of grated nutmeg
2 small eggs		pinch of ground cinnamon
25 g/1 oz/2 tbsp butter, melted	STUFFING:	1 tbsp chopped fresh coriander
pinch of ground cumin	175 g/6 oz minced lamb	(cilantro)
pinch of ground coriander	1 small onion, chopped	2 tbsp lamb stock

1 Put the bulgar wheat in a bowl and cover with boiling water. Soak for 30 minutes until the water has been absorbed and the bulgar wheat has swollen.

2 Meanwhile, cook the diced potatoes in a saucepan of boiling water for 10 minutes or until cooked through. Drain and mash until smooth.

3 Add the bulgar wheat to the mashed potato with the eggs, the melted butter, the ground cumin

and coriander, and the grated nutmeg. Season well with salt and pepper.

4 To make the stuffing, dry fry the lamb for 5 minutes, add the onion and cook for a further 2–3 minutes. Add the remaining stuffing ingredients and cook for 5 minutes until the lamb stock has been absorbed. Leave the mixture to cool slightly, then divide into 8 portions. Roll each one into a ball.

5 Divide the potato mixture into 8 portions and flatten each into a round. Place a portion of stuffing in the centre of each round. Shape the coating around the stuffing to encase it completely.

6 In a large saucepan or deep fat fryer, heat the oil to 180°C–190°C/ 350°F–375°F or until a cube of bread browns in 30 seconds, and cook the kibbeh for 5–7 minutes until golden brown. Drain well and serve at once.

Potato & Meatballs in Spicy Sauce

Serves 4

INGREDIENTS

225 g/8 oz floury (mealy)
    potatoes, diced
225 g/8 oz minced beef or lamb
1 onion, finely chopped
1 tbsp chopped fresh coriander
    (cilantro)
1 celery stick, finely chopped
2 garlic cloves, crushed

25 g/1 oz/2 tbsp butter
1 tbsp vegetable oil
salt and pepper
chopped fresh coriander (cilantro),
    to garnish

SAUCE:
1 tbsp vegetable oil

1 onion, finely chopped
2 tsp soft brown sugar
400 g/14 oz can chopped tomatoes
1 green chilli, chopped
1 tsp paprika
150 ml/¼ pint/⅔ cup vegetable
    stock
2 tsp cornflour (cornstarch)

1 Cook the diced potatoes in a saucepan of boiling water for 25 minutes until cooked through. Drain well and transfer to a large mixing bowl. Mash until smooth.

2 Add the minced beef or lamb, onion, coriander (cilantro), celery and garlic and mix well.

3 Bring the mixture together with your hands and roll it into 20 small balls.

4 To make the sauce, heat the oil in a pan and sauté the onion for 5 minutes. Add the remaining sauce ingredients and bring to the boil, stirring. Lower the heat and simmer for 20 minutes.

5 Meanwhile, heat the butter and oil for the potato and meat balls in a frying pan (skillet). Add the balls in batches and cook for 10–15 minutes until browned, turning frequently. Keep warm whilst cooking the remainder. Serve the potato

and meatballs in a warm shallow ovenproof dish with the sauce poured around them and garnished with coriander (cilantro).

COOK'S TIP

Make the potato and meatballs in advance and chill or freeze them for later use. Make sure you defrost them thoroughly before cooking.

Potato & Mixed Mushroom Cakes

Serves 4

INGREDIENTS

450 g/1lb floury (mealy)
    potatoes, diced
25 g/1 oz/2 tbsp butter
175 g/6 oz mixed mushrooms,
    chopped

2 garlic cloves, crushed
1 small egg, beaten
1 tbsp chopped fresh chives, plus
    extra to garnish
flour, for dusting

oil, for frying
salt and pepper

1 Cook the potatoes in a pan of boiling water for 10 minutes or until cooked through. Drain well, mash and set aside.

2 Meanwhile, melt the butter in a frying pan (skillet) and cook the mushrooms and garlic for 5 minutes, stirring. Drain well.

3 Stir the mushrooms and garlic into the potato together with the beaten egg and chives.

4 Divide the mixture equally into 4 portions and shape them into round cakes. Toss them in the flour until the outside of the cakes is completely coated.

5 Heat the oil in a frying pan (skillet) and cook the potato cakes over a medium heat for 10 minutes until they are golden brown, turning them over halfway through. Serve the cakes at once, with a simple crisp salad.

COOK'S TIP

Prepare the cakes in advance, cover and leave to chill in the refrigerator for up to 24 hours, if you wish.

VARIATION

If chives are unavailable, use other fresh herbs of your choice. Sage, tarragon and coriander (cilantro) all combine well with mixed mushrooms.

Potato Pancakes with Soured Cream & Salmon

Serves 4

INGREDIENTS

450 g/1 lb floury (mealy) potatoes, grated
2 spring onions (scallions), chopped
2 tbsp self-raising flour
2 eggs, beaten

2 tbsp vegetable oil
salt and pepper
fresh chives, to garnish

TOPPING:
150 ml/¼ pint/⅔ cup soured cream
125 g/4½ oz smoked salmon

1 Rinse the grated potatoes under cold running water, drain and pat dry on paper towels. Transfer to a mixing bowl.

2 Mix the chopped spring onions (scallions), flour and eggs into the potatoes and season well with salt and pepper.

3 Heat 1 tbsp of the oil in a frying pan (skillet). Drop about 4 tablespoonfuls of the mixture into the pan and spread each one with the back of a spoon to form a round (the mixture should make 16 pancakes). Cook for 5–7 minutes, turning once, until golden. Drain well.

4 Heat the remaining oil and cook the remaining mixture in batches.

5 Top the pancakes with the soured cream and smoked salmon, garnish with fresh chives and serve hot.

COOK'S TIP

Smaller versions of this dish may be made and served as appetizers.

VARIATION

These pancakes are equally delicious topped with prosciutto or any other dry-cured ham instead of the smoked salmon.

Potato Omelette with Feta Cheese & Spinach

Serves 4

INGREDIENTS

75 g/3 oz/¹⁄₃ cup butter
6 waxy potatoes, diced
3 garlic cloves, crushed
1 tsp paprika

2 tomatoes, skinned, seeded
    and diced
12 eggs
pepper

FILLING:
225 g/8 oz baby spinach
1 tsp fennel seeds
125 g/4¹⁄₂ oz feta cheese, diced
4 tbsp natural yogurt

1 Heat 2 tbsp of the butter in a frying pan (skillet) and cook the potatoes over a low heat for 7–10 minutes until golden, stirring constantly. Transfer to a bowl.

2 Add the garlic, paprika and tomatoes and cook for a further 2 minutes.

3 Whisk the eggs together in a jug and season with pepper. Pour the eggs into the potatoes and mix well.

4 Place the spinach in boiling water for 1 minute until just wilted. Drain and refresh the spinach under cold running water and pat dry with paper towels. Stir in the fennel seeds, feta cheese and yogurt.

5 Heat 1 tbsp of the butter in a 15 cm/6 inch omelette or frying pan (skillet). Ladle a quarter of the egg and potato mixture into the pan. Cook for 2 minutes, turning once, until set.

6 Transfer the omelette to a serving plate. Spoon a quarter of the spinach mixture on to one half of the omelette, then fold the omelette in half over the filling. Repeat to make 4 omelettes.

VARIATION

Use any other cheese, such as blue cheese, instead of the feta and blanched broccoli in place of the baby spinach, if you prefer.

Spanish Tortilla

Serves 4

INGREDIENTS

1 kg/ 2.2 lb waxy potatoes,
thinly sliced
4 tbsp vegetable oil
1 onion, sliced
2 garlic cloves, crushed

1 green (bell) pepper, diced
2 tomatoes, deseeded and
chopped
25 g/1 oz canned sweetcorn,
drained

6 large eggs, beaten
2 tbsp chopped fresh parsley
salt and pepper

1 Parboil the potatoes in a saucepan of boiling water for 5 minutes. Drain well.

2 Heat the oil in a large frying pan (skillet), add the potato and onions and sauté gently for 5 minutes, stirring constantly, until the potatoes have browned.

3 Add the garlic, diced (bell) pepper, chopped tomatoes and sweetcorn, mixing well.

4 Pour in the eggs and add the chopped parsley. Season well with salt and pepper. Cook for 10–12 minutes until the underside is cooked through.

5 Remove the frying pan (skillet) from the heat and continue to cook the tortilla under a preheated medium grill (broiler) for 5–7 minutes or until the tortilla is set and the top is golden brown.

6 Cut the tortilla into wedges or cubes, depending on your preference, and serve with salad. In Spain tortillas are served hot, cold or warm.

COOK'S TIP

Ensure that the handle of your pan is heatproof before placing it under the grill (broiler) and be sure to use an oven glove when removing it as it will be very hot.

Potato & Spinach Filo Triangles

Serves 4

INGREDIENTS

225 g/8 oz waxy potatoes, diced
    finely
450 g/1 lb baby spinach
1 tomato, seeded and chopped
1/4 tsp chilli powder

1/2 tsp lemon juice
225 g/8 oz packet filo pastry,
    thawed if frozen
25 g/1 oz butter, melted
salt and pepper

MAYONNAISE:
150 ml/1/4 pint/2/3 cup
    mayonnaise
2 tsp lemon juice
rind of 1 lemon

1 Lightly grease a baking (cookie) sheet with a little butter.

2 Cook the potatoes in a saucepan of boiling water for 10 minutes or until cooked through. Drain thoroughly and place in a mixing bowl.

3 Meanwhile, put the spinach in a saucepan with 2 tbsp of water, cover and cook over a low heat for 2 minutes until wilted. Drain the spinach thoroughly and add to the potato.

4 Stir in the chopped tomato, chilli powder and lemon juice. Season to taste with salt and pepper.

5 Lightly butter 8 sheets of filo pastry. Spread out 4 of the sheets and lay the other 4 on top of each. Cut them into 20 x 10 cm/ 8 x 4 inch rectangles.

6 Spoon the potato and spinach mixture on to one end of each rectangle. Fold a corner of the pastry over the filling, fold the pointed end back over the pastry strip, then fold over

the remaining pastry to form a triangle.

7 Place the triangles on the baking (cookie) sheet and bake in a preheated oven, 190°C/375°F/Gas Mark 5, for 20 minutes or until golden brown.

8 To make the mayonnaise, mix the mayonnaise, lemon juice and lemon rind together in a small bowl. Serve the potato and spinach filo triangles warm or cold with the lemon mayonnaise and a crisp green salad.

Potatoes with Onion & Herbs

Serves 4

INGREDIENTS

900 g/2 lb waxy potatoes, cut
into cubes
125 g/4¹/₂ oz/¹/₂ cup butter

1 red onion, cut into 8
2 garlic cloves, crushed
1 tsp lemon juice

2 tbsp chopped fresh thyme
salt and pepper

1 Cook the cubed potatoes in a saucepan of boiling water for 10 minutes. Drain thoroughly.

2 Melt the butter in a large, heavy-based frying pan (skillet) and add the red onion wedges, garlic and lemon juice. Cook for 2–3 minutes, stirring.

3 Add the potatoes to the pan and mix well to coat in the butter mixture.

4 Reduce the heat, cover the frying pan (skillet) and cook for 25–30 minutes or until the potatoes are golden and tender.

5 Sprinkle the chopped thyme over the top of the potatoes and season with salt and pepper to taste.

6 Serve immediately as a side dish to accompany grilled meats or fish.

COOK'S TIP

Keep checking the potatoes and stirring throughout the cooking time to ensure that they do not burn or stick to the bottom of the frying pan (skillet).

COOK'S TIP

Onions are used in a multitude of dishes to which they add their pungent flavour. The beautifully coloured purple-red onions used here have a mild, slightly sweet flavour as well as looking extremely attractive. Because of their mild taste, they are equally good eaten raw in salads.

Spicy Indian Potatoes with Spinach

Serves 4

INGREDIENTS

¹/₂ tsp coriander seeds
1 tsp cumin seeds
4 tbsp vegetable oil
2 cardamon pods
1 cm/¹/₂ inch piece ginger
    root, grated

1 red chilli, chopped
1 onion, chopped
2 garlic cloves, crushed
450 g/1 lb new potatoes,
    quartered
675 g/1¹/₂ lb spinach, chopped

150 ml/¹/₄ pint/²/₃ cup vegetable
    stock
4 tbsp natural yogurt
salt

1 Grind the coriander and cumin seeds using a pestle and mortar.

2 Heat the oil in a frying pan (skillet). Add the ground coriander and cumin seeds to the pan together with the cardamom pods and ginger and cook for about 2 minutes.

3 Add the chopped chilli, onion and garlic to the pan. Cook for a further 2 minutes, stirring frequently

4 Add the potatoes to the pan together with the vegetable stock. Cook gently for 30 minutes or until the potatoes are cooked through, stirring occasionally.

5 Add the spinach to the pan and cook for a further 5 minutes.

6 Remove the pan from the heat and stir in the yogurt. Season with salt and pepper to taste. Transfer the potatoes and spinach to a serving dish and serve.

COOK'S TIP

This spicy dish is ideal served with a meat curry or alternatively, as part of a vegetarian meal.

VARIATION

Use frozen spinach instead of fresh spinach, if you prefer. Defrost the frozen spinach and drain it thoroughly before adding it to the dish, otherwise it will turn soggy.

Potatoes & Mushrooms in Red Wine

Serves 4

INGREDIENTS

125 g/4¹/2 oz/¹/2 cup butter
450 g/1 lb new potatoes, halved
200 ml/7 fl oz/³/4 cup red wine
85 ml/3 fl oz/¹/3 cup beef stock

8 shallots, halved
125 g/4¹/2 oz oyster mushrooms
1 tbsp chopped fresh sage or
    coriander (cilantro)

salt and pepper
sage leaves or coriander
    (cilantro) sprigs, to garnish

1 Melt the butter in a heavy-based frying pan (skillet) and add the halved potatoes. Cook gently for 5 minutes, stirring constantly.

2 Add the red wine, beef stock and halved shallots. Season to taste with salt and pepper and then simmer for 30 minutes.

3 Stir in the mushrooms and chopped sage or coriander (cilantro) and cook for 5 minutes.

4 Turn the potatoes and mushrooms into a warm serving dish. Garnish with sage leaves or coriander (cilantro) sprigs and serve at once.

VARIATION

If oyster mushrooms are unavailable, other mushrooms, such as large open cap mushrooms, can be used instead.

COOK'S TIP

Oyster mushrooms may be grey, yellow or red in colour. They have a soft, melting texture and mild flavour. As they cook, they emit a lot of liquid and shrink to about half their original size. They require little cooking before they start to turn mushy, so add them at the end of the cooking time.

Spicy Potato Fries

Serves 4

INGREDIENTS

4 large waxy potatoes 2 sweet potatoes	50 g/1¾ oz/4 tbsp butter, melted ½ tsp chilli powder	1 tsp garam masala salt

1 Cut the potatoes and sweet potatoes into slices about 1 cm/½ inch thick, then cut them into chip shapes.

2 Place the potatoes in a large bowl of cold salted water. Leave to soak for 20 minutes.

3 Remove the potato slices with a perforated spoon and drain thoroughly. Pat with paper towels until completely dry.

4 Pour the melted butter on to a baking (cookie) sheet. Transfer the potato slices to the baking (cookie) sheet. Sprinkle with the chilli powder and garam masala, turning the potato slices to coat them with the mixture.

5 Cook the chips in a preheated oven, 200°C/400°F/Gas Mark 6, for 40 minutes, turning frequently until browned and cooked through.

6 Drain the chips on paper towels to remove the excess oil and serve at once.

COOK'S TIP

Rinsing the potatoes in cold water before cooking removes the starch, thus preventing them from sticking together. Soaking the potatoes in a bowl of cold salted water actually makes the cooked chips crisper.

VARIATION

For added flavour, sprinkle the chips with fennel seeds or cumin seeds, before serving.

Italian Potato Wedges

Serves 4

INGREDIENTS

2 large waxy potatoes, unpeeled
4 large ripe tomatoes, peeled and
    seeded
150 ml/¼ pint/⅔ cup vegetable
    stock

2 tbsp tomato purée (paste)
1 small yellow (bell) pepper, cut
    into strips
125 g/4½ oz button mushrooms,
    quartered

1 tbsp chopped fresh basil
50 g/1¾ oz cheese, grated
salt and pepper

1 Cut each of the potatoes into 8 equal wedges. Parboil the potatoes in a pan of boiling water for 15 minutes. Drain well and place in a shallow ovenproof dish.

2 Chop the tomatoes and add to the dish. Mix together the vegetable stock and tomato purée (paste), then pour the mixture over the potatoes and tomatoes.

3 Add the yellow (bell) pepper strips, quartered mushrooms and chopped basil. Season well with salt and pepper.

4 Sprinkle the grated cheese over the top and cook in a preheated oven, 190°C/375°F/Gas Mark 5, for 15–20 minutes until the topping is golden brown. Serve at once.

COOK'S TIP

For the topping, use any cheese that melts well, such as Mozzarella, the traditional pizza cheese. Alternatively, you could use either Gruyère or Emmental cheese, if you prefer.

VARIATION

These potato wedges can also be served as a light supper dish, accompanied by chunks of crusty, fresh brown or white bread.

Potatoes Dauphinois

Serves 4

INGREDIENTS

15 g/¹/₂ oz/1 tbsp butter
675 g/1¹/₂ lb waxy potatoes,
   sliced

2 garlic cloves, crushed
1 red onion, sliced
75 g/3 oz Gruyère cheese, grated

300 ml/¹/₂ pint/1¹/₄ cups double
   (heavy) cream
salt and pepper

1 Lightly grease a
1 litre/1³/₄ pint/4 cup
shallow ovenproof dish with
a little butter.

2 Arrange a single layer
of potato slices in the
base of the prepared dish.

3 Top the potato slices
with a little of the garlic,
sliced red onion and grated
Gruyére cheese. Season to
taste with a little salt and
pepper.

4 Repeat the layers in
exactly the same order,
finishing with a layer of
potatoes topped with cheese.

5 Pour the cream over
the top of the potatoes
and cook in a preheated
oven, 180°C/350°F/Gas
Mark 4, for 1¹/₂ hours or
until the potatoes are cooked
through, browned and
crispy. Serve at once.

COOK'S TIP

*Add a layer of chopped
bacon or ham to this dish,
if you prefer, and serve with
a crisp green salad for a
light supper.*

VARIATION

*There are many versions of
this classic potato dish, but
the different recipes always
contain double (heavy)
cream, making it a rich and
very filling side dish or
accompaniment. This recipe
must be cooked in a shallow
dish to ensure there is plenty
of crispy topping.*

Potatoes with Almonds & Cream

Serves 4

INGREDIENTS

2 large potatoes, unpeeled and sliced	50 g/1³/₄ oz almond flakes	1 garlic clove, crushed
1 tbsp vegetable oil	¹/₂ tsp turmeric	125 g/4¹/₂ oz rocket (arugula)
1 red onion, halved and sliced	300ml/¹/₂ pint/1¹/₄ cups double (heavy) cream	salt and pepper

1 Cook the sliced potatoes in a saucepan of boiling water for 10 minutes. Drain thoroughly.

2 Heat the vegetable oil in a frying pan (skillet) and cook the onion and garlic for 3–4 minutes, stirring frequently.

3 Add the almonds, turmeric and potato slices to the frying pan (skillet) and cook for 2–3 minutes, stirring constantly. Stir in the rocket (arugula).

4 Transfer the potato and almond mixture to a shallow ovenproof dish. Pour the double (heavy) cream over the top and season with salt and pepper.

5 Cook in a preheated oven, 190°C/375°F/ Gas Mark 5, for 20 minutes or until the potatoes are cooked through. Serve as an accompaniment to grilled (broiled) meat or fish dishes.

VARIATION

You could use other nuts, such as unsalted peanuts or cashews, instead of the almond flakes, if you prefer.

VARIATION

If rocket (arugula) is unavailable, use the same quantity of trimmed baby spinach instead.

Cheese Crumble-Topped Mash

Serves 4

INGREDIENTS

900 g/2 lb floury (mealy)
potatoes, diced
25 g/1 oz/2 tbsp butter
2 tbsp milk
50 g/1³/₄ oz mature (sharp)
cheese or blue cheese, grated

CRUMBLE TOPPING:
40 g/1¹/₂ oz/3 tbsp butter
1 onion, cut into chunks
1 garlic clove, crushed
1 tbsp wholegrain mustard

175 g/ 6 oz/3 cups fresh
wholemeal (whole wheat)
breadcrumbs
2 tbsp chopped fresh parsley
salt and pepper .

1 Cook the potatoes in a pan of boiling water for 10 minutes or until cooked through.

2 Meanwhile, make the crumble topping. Melt the butter in a frying pan (skillet). Add the onion, garlic and mustard and fry gently for 5 minutes until the onion chunks have softened, stirring constantly.

3 Put the breadcrumbs in a mixing bowl and stir in the fried onion. Season to taste with salt and pepper.

4 Drain the potatoes thoroughly and place them in a mixing bowl. Add the butter and milk, then mash until smooth. Stir in the grated cheese while the potato is still hot.

5 Spoon the mashed potato into a shallow ovenproof dish and sprinkle with the crumble topping.

6 Cook in a preheated oven, 200°C/400°F/ Gas Mark 6, for 10–15 minutes until the crumble topping is golden brown and crunchy. Serve immediately.

COOK'S TIP

For extra crunch, add freshly cooked vegetables, such as celery and (bell) peppers, to the mashed potato in step 4.

Lamb Hotpot

Serves 4

INGREDIENTS

675 g/1½ lb best end of lamb
    neck cutlets
2 lamb's kidneys
1 large onion, sliced thinly

675 g/1½ lb waxy potatoes,
    scrubbed and sliced thinly
2 tbsp chopped fresh thyme
150 ml/¼ pint/⅔ cup lamb stock

25 g/1 oz/2 tbsp butter, melted
salt and pepper
fresh thyme sprigs, to garnish

1 Remove any excess fat from the lamb. Skin and core the kidneys and cut them into slices.

2 Arrange a layer of potatoes in the base of a 1.8 litre/3 pint/3½ cup ovenproof dish.

3 Arrange the lamb neck cutlets on top of the potatoes and cover with the sliced kidneys, onion and chopped fresh thyme.

4 Pour the lamb stock over the meat and season to taste with salt and pepper.

5 Layer the remaining potato slices on top, overlapping to completely cover the meat and sliced onion.

6 Brush the potato slices with the butter, cover the dish and cook in a preheated oven, 180°C/ 350°F/ Gas Mark 4, for 1½ hours.

7 Remove the lid and cook for a further 30 minutes until golden brown on top.

8 Garnish with fresh thyme sprigs and serve hot.

COOK'S TIP

Although this is a classic recipe, extra ingredients of your choice, such as celery or carrots, can be added to the dish for variety and colour.

VARIATION

Traditionally, oysters are also included in this tasty hotpot. Add them to the layers along with the kidneys, if wished.

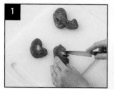

Potato, Tomato & Sausage Panfry

Serves 4

INGREDIENTS

2 large potatoes, sliced
1 tbsp vegetable oil
8 flavoured sausages
1 red onion, cut into 8
1 tbsp tomato purée (paste)

150 ml/¼ pint/⅔ cup red wine
150 ml/¼ pint/⅔ cup passata
2 large tomatoes, each cut into 8
175 g/6 oz broccoli florets,
  blanched

2 tbsp chopped fresh basil
salt and pepper
shredded fresh basil, to garnish

1 Cook the sliced potatoes in a saucepan of boiling water for 7 minutes. Drain thoroughly and set aside.

2 Meanwhile, heat the oil in a large frying pan (skillet). Add the sausages and cook for 5 minutes, turning the sausages frequently to ensure that they are browned on all sides.

3 Add the onion pieces to the pan and continue to cook for a further 5 minutes, stirring the mixture frequently.

4 Stir in the tomato purée (paste), red wine and the passata and mix together well. Add the tomato wedges, broccoli florets and chopped basil to the panfry and mix carefully.

5 Add the parboiled potato slices to the pan. Cook the mixture for about 10 minutes or until the sausages are completely cooked through. Season to taste with salt and pepper.

6 Garnish the panfry with fresh shredded basil and serve hot.

COOK'S TIP

Omit the passata from this recipe and use canned plum tomatoes or chopped tomatoes for convenience.

VARIATION

Broccoli is particularly good in this dish as it adds a splash of colour, but other vegetables of your choice can be used instead, if preferred.

Potato Curry

Serves 4

INGREDIENTS

4 tbsp vegetable oil
675 g/1½ lb waxy potatoes, cut into large chunks
2 onions, quartered
3 garlic cloves, crushed
1 tsp garam masala
½ tsp turmeric

½ tsp ground cumin
½ tsp ground coriander
2.5 cm/1 inch piece ginger root, grated
1 red chilli, chopped
225 g/8 oz cauliflower florets
4 tomatoes, peeled and quartered

75 g/2¾ oz frozen peas
2 tbsp chopped fresh coriander (cilantro)
300 ml/½ pint/1¼ cups vegetable stock
shredded fresh coriander (cilantro), to garnish

1 Heat the vegetable oil in a large heavy-based saucepan or frying pan (skillet). Add the potato chunks, onion and garlic and fry gently for 2–3 minutes, stirring the mixture frequently.

2 Add the garam masala, turmeric, ground cumin, ground coriander, grated ginger and chopped chilli to the pan, mixing the spices into the vegetables. Fry for 1 minute, stirring constantly.

3 Add the cauliflower florets, tomatoes, peas, chopped coriander (cilantro) and vegetable stock to the curry mixture.

4 Cook the potato curry over a low heat for 30–40 minutes or until the potatoes are completely cooked through.

5 Garnish the potato curry with fresh coriander (cilantro) and serve with plain boiled rice or warm Indian bread.

COOK'S TIP

Use a large heavy-based saucepan or frying pan (skillet) for this recipe to ensure that the potatoes are cooked thoroughly.

Potato & Spinach Gnocchi

Serves 4

INGREDIENTS

300 g/10¹/₂ oz floury (mealy)
  potatoes, diced
175 g/6 oz spinach
125 g/4¹/₂ oz/1 cup plain
  (all-purpose) flour
1 egg yolk

1 tsp olive oil
salt and pepper
spinach leaves, to garnish

SAUCE:
1 tbsp olive oil
2 shallots, chopped
1 garlic clove, crushed
300 ml/¹/₂ pint/1¹/₄ cups passata
2 tsp soft light brown sugar

1 Cook the diced potatoes in a saucepan of boiling water for 10 minutes until cooked through. Drain and mash the potatoes.

2 Meanwhile, in a separate pan, blanch the spinach in a little boiling water for 1–2 minutes. Drain well and shred the leaves.

3 Transfer the mashed potato to a lightly floured chopping board and make a well in the centre. Add the egg yolk, olive oil, spinach and a little of the flour and quickly mix the ingredients into the potato, adding more flour as you go, until you have a firm dough. Divide the mixture into very small dumplings.

4 Cook the gnocchi in batches in a saucepan of boiling salted water for about 5 minutes or until they rise to the top of the pan.

5 Meanwhile, make the sauce. Put the oil, shallots, garlic, passata and sugar into a saucepan and cook over a low heat for 10–15 minutes or until the sauce has thickened.

6 Drain the gnocchi using a perforated spoon and transfer to warm serving dishes. Spoon the sauce over the gnocchi and garnish with the fresh spinach leaves.

VARIATION

Add chopped fresh herbs and cheese to the gnocchi dough instead of the spinach, if you prefer.

Potato & Three Cheese Soufflé

Serves 4

INGREDIENTS

25 g/1 oz/2 tbsp butter
2 tsp plain (all-purpose) flour
900 g/2 lb floury (mealy)
   potatoes

8 eggs, separated
25 g/1 oz Gruyère cheese, grated
25 g/1 oz mature (sharp) cheese,
   grated

25 g/1 oz blue cheese, crumbled
salt and pepper

1 Butter a 2.4 litre/4 pint/
10 cup soufflé dish and
dust with the flour. Set aside.

2 Cook the potatoes in
a saucepan of boiling
water until cooked through.
Mash until very smooth
and transfer to a mixing
bowl to cool.

3 Whisk the egg
yolks into the potato
and stir in the 3 different
cheeses. Season well with
salt and pepper.

4 In a clean bowl, whisk
the egg whites until
standing in peaks, then gently
fold them into the potato
mixture with a metal spoon
until fully incorporated.

5 Spoon the potato
mixture into the
prepared soufflé dish.

6 Cook in a preheated
oven, 220°C/425°F/
Gas Mark 7, for 35–40
minutes until risen and set.
Serve immediately.

COOK'S TIP

*Insert a fine skewer into
the centre of the soufflé; it
should come out clean
when the soufflé is fully
cooked through.*

VARIATION

*You can add chopped cooked
bacon to the soufflé for extra
flavour, if wished.*

Vegetable Cake

Serves 4

INGREDIENTS

BASE:
2 tbsp vegetable oil
4 large waxy potatoes, sliced thinly

TOPPING:
1 tbsp vegetable oil

1 leek, chopped
1 courgette (zucchini), grated
1 red (bell) pepper, diced
1 green (bell) pepper, diced
1 carrot, grated
2 tsp chopped fresh parsley

225 g/8 oz full fat soft cheese
25 g/1 oz mature (sharp) cheese, grated
2 eggs, beaten
salt and pepper
shredded cooked leek, to garnish

---

1 Grease a 20 cm/8 inch springform cake tin (pan).

2 To make the base, heat the oil in a frying pan (skillet). Cook the potato slices in batches over a medium heat until softened and browned. Drain thoroughly on paper towels and arrange the slices in the base of the tin (pan).

3 To make the topping, heat the oil in a separate frying pan (skillet) and fry the leek over a low heat for 3–4 minutes until softened.

4 Add the courgette (zucchini), (bell) peppers, carrot and parsley to the pan and cook over a low heat for 5–7 minutes or until the vegetables have softened.

5 Meanwhile, beat the cheeses and eggs together in a bowl. Stir in the vegetables and season to taste with salt and pepper. Spoon the mixture on to the potato base.

6 Cook in a preheated oven, 190°C/375°F/ Gas Mark 5, for 20–25 minutes until the cake is set.

7 Remove the vegetable cake from the tin (pan), garnish with shredded leek and serve with a crisp salad.

COOK'S TIP

Add diced tofu (bean curd) or diced meat, such as pork or chicken, to the topping, if wished. Cook the meat with the vegetables in step 4.

Bubble & Squeak

Serves 4

INGREDIENTS

450 g/1 lb floury (mealy)
potatoes, diced
225 g/8 oz Savoy cabbage,
shredded
5 tbsp vegetable oil

2 leeks, chopped
1 garlic clove, crushed
225 g/8 oz smoked tofu
(bean curd), cubed

salt and pepper
shredded cooked leek, to garnish

1 Cook the diced potatoes in a saucepan of boiling water for 10 minutes until tender. Drain and mash the potatoes.

2 Meanwhile, in a separate saucepan blanch the cabbage in boiling water for 5 minutes. Drain and add to the potato.

3 Heat the oil in a heavy-based frying pan (skillet), add the leeks and garlic and fry gently for 2–3 minutes. Stir into the potato and cabbage mixture.

4 Add the smoked tofu (bean curd) and season well with salt and pepper. Cook over a moderate heat for 10 minutes.

5 Carefully turn the whole mixture over and continue to cook over a moderate heat for a further 5–7 minutes until crispy underneath. Serve immediately, garnished with shredded leek.

VARIATION

You can add cooked meats, such as beef or chicken, instead of the tofu (bean curd) for a more traditional recipe. Any gravy from the cooked meats can also be added, but ensure that the mixture is not too wet.

COOK'S TIP

This vegetarian recipe is a perfect main meal, as the smoked tofu (bean curd) cubes added to the basic bubble and squeak mixture make it very substantial.

Twice-Baked Potatoes with Pesto

Serves 4

| INGREDIENTS |

4 baking potatoes, about 225 g/
    8 oz each
150 ml/¼ pint/²/₃ cup double
    (heavy) cream
1 tbsp lemon juice

2 garlic cloves, crushed
85 ml/3 fl oz/¹/₃ cup
    vegetable stock
3 tbsp chopped fresh basil
2 tbsp pine kernels (nuts)

2 tbsp grated Parmesan cheese
salt and pepper

1 Scrub the potatoes and prick the skins with a fork. Rub a little salt into the skins and place on a baking (cookie) sheet.

2 Cook in a preheated oven, 190°C/375°F/ Gas Mark 5, for 1 hour or until the potatoes are cooked through and the skins crisp.

3 Remove the potatoes from the oven and cut them in half lengthways. Using a spoon, scoop the potato flesh into a mixing bowl, leaving a thin shell of potato inside the skins. Mash the potato flesh with a fork.

4 Meanwhile, mix the cream and stock in a saucepan and simmer for 8–10 minutes or until reduced by half.

5 Stir in the lemon juice, garlic and chopped basil and season to taste with salt and pepper. Stir the mixture into the potato flesh with the pine kernels (nuts).

6 Spoon the mixture back into the potato shells and sprinkle the Parmesan cheese on top. Return the potatoes to the oven for 10 minutes or until the cheese has browned. Serve with fresh salad.

VARIATION

Add full fat soft cheese or thinly sliced mushrooms to the mashed potato flesh in step 5, if you prefer.

Potato & Aubergine (Eggplant) Gratin

Serves 4

INGREDIENTS

450 g/1/lb waxy potatoes, sliced

1 tbsp vegetable oil

1 onion, chopped

2 garlic cloves, crushed

450 g/1 lb tofu (bean curd), diced

2 tbsp tomato purée (paste)

2 tbsp plain (all-purpose) flour

300 ml/1/2 pint/1 1/4 cups
    vegetable stock

2 large tomatoes, sliced

1 aubergine (eggplant), sliced

2 tbsp chopped fresh thyme

450 g/1/lb natural yogurt

2 eggs, beaten

salt and pepper

---

1 Cook the sliced potatoes in a saucepan of boiling water for 10 minutes until tender but not breaking up. Drain and set aside.

2 Heat the oil in a pan and fry the onion and garlic for 2–3 minutes.

3 Add the diced tofu (bean curd), tomato purée (paste) and flour and cook for 1 minute. Gradually stir in the vegetable stock and bring to the boil, stirring constantly. Reduce the heat and leave to simmer for 10 minutes.

4 Arrange a layer of the potato slices in the base of a deep ovenproof dish. Spoon the tofu (bean curd) mixture on top.

5 Layer the tomatoes, then the aubergine (eggplant) and then the remaining potato slices on top of the tofu mixture, making sure that it is completely covered.

6 Mix the yogurt and beaten eggs together in a bowl and season well with salt and pepper. Spoon the yogurt topping over the sliced potatoes.

7 Cook in a preheated oven, 190°C/375°F/ Gas Mark 5, for 35–45 minutes or until the topping is browned. Serve hot, with a crisp green salad.

VARIATION

You can use marinated or smoked tofu (bean curd) for extra flavour, if you wish.

Potato & Tomato Calzone

Makes 4

INGREDIENTS

DOUGH: 450 g/1 lb/4 cups white bread flour 1 tsp easy blend dried yeast 300 ml/¹/₂ pint/1¹/₄ cups vegetable stock 1 tbsp clear honey	1 tsp caraway seeds milk, for glazing FILLING: 225 g/8 oz waxy potatoes, diced 1 tbsp vegetable oil 1 onion, halved and sliced	2 garlic cloves, crushed 40 g/1¹/₂ oz sun-dried tomatoes 2 tbsp chopped fresh basil 2 tbsp tomato purée (paste) 2 celery sticks, sliced 50 g/2 oz Mozzarella cheese, grated

1 To make the dough, sift the flour into a large mixing bowl and stir in the yeast. Make a well in the centre of the mixture.

2 Stir in the vegetable stock, honey and caraway seeds and bring the mixture together to form a dough.

3 Turn the dough out on to a lightly floured surface and knead for 8 minutes until smooth. Place the dough in a lightly oiled mixing bowl, cover and leave to rise in a warm place for 1 hour or until it has doubled in size.

4 Meanwhile, make the filling. Heat the oil in a frying pan (skillet) and add all the remaining ingredients except for the cheese. Cook for about 5 minutes, stirring.

5 Divide the risen dough into 4 pieces. On a lightly floured surface, roll them out to form four 18 cm/7 inch circles. Spoon equal amounts of the filling on to one half of each circle.

6 Sprinkle the cheese over the filling. Brush the edge of the dough with milk and fold the dough over to form 4 semi-circles, pressing to seal the edges.

7 Place on a non-stick baking (cookie) sheet and brush with milk. Cook in a preheated oven, 220°C/425°F/Gas Mark 7, for 30 minutes until golden and risen.

Potato & Broccoli Pie

Serves 4

INGREDIENTS

450 g/1 lb waxy potatoes, cut into chunks	25 g/1 oz plain (all-purpose) flour	175 g/6 oz broccoli florets
25 g/1 oz/2 tbsp butter	150 ml/$\frac{1}{4}$ pint/$\frac{2}{3}$ cup vegetable stock	25 g/1 oz walnuts
1 tbsp vegetable oil	150 ml/$\frac{1}{4}$ pint/$\frac{2}{3}$ cup milk	225 g/8 oz ready-made puff pastry (pie dough)
175 g/6 oz lean pork, cubed	75 g/2$\frac{3}{4}$ oz dolcelatte, crumbled	milk, for glazing
1 red onion, cut into 8		salt and pepper

1 Cook the potato chunks in a saucepan of boiling water for 5 minutes. Drain and set aside.

2 Meanwhile, heat the butter and oil in a heavy-based pan. Add the pork cubes and cook for 5 minutes, turning until browned.

3 Add the onion and cook for a further 2 minutes. Stir in the flour and cook for 1 minute, then gradually stir in the vegetable stock and milk. Bring to the boil, stirring constantly.

4 Add the cheese, broccoli, potatoes and walnuts to the pan and simmer for 5 minutes. Season with salt and pepper, then spoon the mixture into a pie dish.

5 On a floured surface, roll out the pastry (pie dough) until 2.5 cm/ 1 inch larger than the dish. Cut a 2.5 cm/1 inch wide strip from the pastry (pie dough). Dampen the edge of the dish and place the pastry (pie dough) strip around it. Brush with milk and put the pastry (pie dough) lid on top.

6 Seal and crimp the edges and make 2 small slits in the centre of the lid. Brush with milk and cook in a preheated oven, 200°C/400°F/Gas Mark 6, for 25 minutes or until the pastry has risen and is golden.

COOK'S TIP

Use a hard cheese such as mature (sharp) cheese instead of the dolcelatte, if you prefer.

Potato-Topped Smoked Fish Pie

Serves 4

INGREDIENTS

450 g/1 lb floury (mealy)
  potatoes, diced
225 g/8 oz swede, diced
60 g/2 oz/¼ cup butter
1 leek, sliced
50 g/1¾ oz baby sweetcorn
  cobs, sliced
1 courgette (zucchini), halved
  and sliced

50 g/1¾ oz/⅓ cup plain
  (all-purpose) flour
300 ml/½ pint/1¼ cups milk
150 ml/¼ pint/⅔ cup fish stock
150 ml/¼ pint/⅔ cup double
  (heavy) cream
450 g/1 lb smoked cod fillet, cut
  into cubes
few drops of Tabasco sauce

125 g/4½ oz cooked peeled
  prawns (shrimp)
2 tbsp chopped fresh parsley
2 tbsp grated Parmesan cheese
salt and pepper

1 Cook the potatoes and swede in a saucepan of boiling water for 20 minutes until very tender. Drain and mash until smooth.

2 Meanwhile, melt the butter in a saucepan, add the leeks, sweetcorn cobs and courgette (zucchini) and fry gently for 3–4 minutes, stirring.

3 Add the flour and cook for 1 minute. Gradually blend in the milk, fish stock and cream and bring to the boil, stirring until the mixture begins to thicken.

4 Stir in the fish, reduce the heat and cook for 5 minutes. Add the Tabasco sauce, prawns (shrimp), half of the parsley and season. Spoon the mixture into the base of an ovenproof dish.

5 Mix the remaining parsley into the potato and swede mixture, season and spoon or pipe on to the fish mixture, covering it completely. Sprinkle with the grated cheese and cook in a preheated oven, 180°C/350°F/Gas Mark 4, for 20 minutes. Serve the pie immediately.

VARIATION

Add cooked mashed parsnip to the potato instead of the swede.

Potato & Aubergine (Eggplant) Layer

Serves 4

INGREDIENTS

3 large waxy potatoes, sliced thinly	1 green (bell) pepper, diced	225 g/8 oz tofu (bean curd), sliced
1 small aubergine (eggplant), sliced thinly	1 tsp cumin seeds	60 g/2 oz/1 cup fresh white breadcrumbs
1 courgette (zucchini), sliced	200 g/7 oz can chopped tomatoes	2 tbsp grated Parmesan cheese
2 tbsp vegetable oil	2 tbsp chopped fresh basil	salt and pepper
1 onion, diced	175 g/6 oz Mozzarella cheese, sliced	fresh basil leaves, to garnish

1 Cook the sliced potatoes in a saucepan of boiling water for 5 minutes. Drain and set aside.

2 Lay the aubergine (eggplant) slices on a plate, sprinkle with salt and leave for 20 minutes. Blanch the courgette (zucchini) in boiling water for 2–3 minutes. Drain and set aside.

3 Meanwhile, heat 2 tbsp of the oil in a frying pan (skillet), add the onion and fry gently for 2–3 minutes until softened. Add the (bell) pepper, cumin seeds, basil and canned tomatoes. Season with salt and pepper. Leave the sauce to simmer for 30 minutes.

4 Rinse the aubergine (eggplant) slices and pat dry. Heat the remaining oil in a large frying pan (skillet) and fry the aubergine (eggplant) slices for 3–5 minutes, turning to brown both sides. Drain and set aside.

5 Arrange half of the potato slices in the base of 4 small loose-bottomed flan tins (pans). Cover with half of the courgette (zucchini) slices, half of the aubergine (eggplant) slices and half of the Mozzarella slices. Lay the tofu (bean curd) on top and spoon over the tomato sauce. Repeat the layers of vegetables and cheese.

6 Mix the breadcrumbs and Parmesan together and sprinkle over the top. Cook in a preheated oven, 190°C/375°F/Gas Mark 5, for 25–30 minutes or until golden. Garnish with basil leaves.

Potato & Nutmeg Scones

Makes 8

INGREDIENTS

225 g/8 oz floury (mealy)
potatoes, diced

125 g/4½ oz/1 cup plain
(all-purpose) flour

1½ tsp baking powder

½ tsp grated nutmeg

50 g/1¾ oz/⅓ cup sultanas
(golden raisins)

1 egg, beaten

50 ml/2 fl oz/¼ cup double
(heavy) cream

2 tsp soft light brown sugar

1 Line and grease a baking (cookie) sheet.

2 Cook the diced potatoes in a saucepan of boiling water for 10 minutes or until soft. Drain well and mash the potatoes.

3 Transfer the mashed potatoes to a large mixing bowl and stir in the flour, baking powder and nutmeg.

4 Stir in the sultanas (golden raisins), egg and cream and beat the mixture with a spoon until smooth.

5 Shape the mixture into 8 rounds 2 cm/¾ inch thick and put on the baking (cookie) sheet.

6 Cook in a preheated oven, 200°C/400°F/Gas Mark 6, for about 15 minutes or until the scones have risen and are golden. Sprinkle the scones with sugar and serve warm and spread with butter.

COOK'S TIP

For extra convenience, make a batch of scones in advance and open-freeze them. Thaw thoroughly and warm in a moderate oven when ready to serve.

VARIATION

This recipe may be used to make one large scone 'cake' instead of the 8 small scones, if you prefer.

Potato Muffins

Serves 12

INGREDIENTS

175 g/6 oz floury (mealy)
potatoes, diced
75 g/3 oz/³/4 cup self raising flour

2 tbsp soft light brown sugar
1 tsp baking powder

125 g/4¹/2 oz/³/4 cup raisins
4 eggs, separated

1 Lightly grease and flour 12 muffin tins (pans).

2 Cook the diced potatoes in a saucepan of boiling water for 10 minutes or until cooked. Drain well and mash until smooth.

3 Transfer the mashed potatoes to a mixing bowl and add the flour, sugar, baking powder, raisins and egg yolks. Stir well to mix thoroughly.

4 In a clean bowl, whisk the egg whites until standing in peaks. Using a metal spoon, gently fold them into the potato mixture until fully incorporated.

5 Divide the mixture between the prepared tins (pans).

6 Cook in a preheated oven, 200°C/400°F/ Gas Mark 6, for 10 minutes. Reduce the oven temperature to 160°C/325°F/Gas Mark 3 and cook the muffins for 7–10 minutes or until risen.

7 Remove the muffins from the tins (pans) and serve warm.

COOK'S TIP

Instead of spreading the muffins with plain butter, serve them with cinnamon butter made by blending 60 g/2 oz/¹/2 cup butter with a large pinch of ground cinnamon.

VARIATION

Other flavourings, such as cinnamon or nutmeg, can be added to the mixture, if you prefer.